ROYAL COUF

The Royal Court Theatre preser

KIN

by **E.V. Crowe**

First performance at the Royal Court Jerwood Theatre Upstairs, Sloane Square,
London on Friday 19 November 2010.

KIN

by E.V Crowe

(in order of appearance)
Janey **Mimi Keene, Madison Lygo**
Mimi **Maya Gerber, Ciara Southwood**
Mrs B **Annette Badland**
Nina **Fern Deacon, Ellen Hill**
Mr Thorne **Kevin McMonagle**
Marcus **Ollie Barbieri**

Director **Jeremy Herrin**
Designer **Bunny Christie**
Lighting Designer **Malcolm Rippeth**
Sound Designer **Christopher Shutt**
Casting Director **Julia Horan**
Assistant Director **Manal Awad**
Production Manager **Tariq Rifaat**
Stage Managers **Pin Dix & Fran O'Donnell**
Fight Director **Kate Waters**
Costume Supervisor **Iona Kenrick**
Stage Management Work Placement **Claire Baldwin**
Set built by **Object Construction Ltd & Richard Martin**
Set painted by **Jodie Pritchard**

The Royal Court and Stage Management would like to thank the following for their help with this production: Almeida Theatre, Architectural Forum, Sarah Davies, Donmar Warehouse, Guildhall School of Music and Drama, Majella Hurley, Hampstead Theatre, LAMDA, David McSeveney, PHS Group Ltd, Royal School Hampstead.

THE COMPANY

E.V. CROWE (Writer)

FOR THE ROYAL COURT: One Runs the Other Doesn't (Hung Over - Election Shorts Rough Cut).

UPCOMING PRODUCTIONS: Live Feed, I'm Going to Show You (as part of ROTOR, Siobhan Davies Studios); Doris Day (as part of Charged, Clean Break at Soho Theatre)

E V Crowe was a member of the Royal Court Young Writers Programme and has been on attachment at the Royal Court, Summer 2007 and National Theatre Studio, Summer 2010.

MANAL AWAD (Assistant Director)

AS DIRECTOR, THEATRE INCLUDES: 603 (Haya Theatre, Palestine); Junín Dementia (RADA).

AS ACTRESS THEATRE INCLUDES: Gaza – Ramallah (Haya Theatre); The Doll's House, Blood Wedding, The Wall, Cell 76, Regulate Your Watches, Something about Rumaneh, Cinderella, The Emperor's New Clothes, The Nightingale (AL Kasaba Theatre, Ramallah); Miladeh and Ramadan, Little Match Girl (Inad Theatre, Palestine).

AS ACTRESS TELEVISION & FILM INCLUDES: Homeland on String, The Pomegranate and Myrrh, The Occupied, Jerusalem in Another Day, Speed Bump.

Manal is a currently doing her MA Theatre Directing at The Royal Academy of Dramatic Art, London.

ANNETTE BADLAND (Mrs B)

FOR THE ROYAL COURT: Hungover Election Shorts (Rough Cut); The Kitchen.

OTHER THEATRE INCLUDES: Far Away (Bristol Old Vic); Blithe Spirit (Manchester Royal Exchange); The Vortex (West End); Grumpy Old Women Live (Tour); Habeus Corpus, Measure for Measure (Theatre Royal Bath); 'Tis Pity She's a Whore, The Daughter in Law, Dr Faustus, Romeo and Juliet, Small Ads (Young Vic); The Prime of Miss Jean Brodie, The Rise and Fall of Little Voice (National/West End); A Midsummer Night's Dream (Leicester); Slavs (Hampstead); Brighton Beach Scumbags (Riverside Studios); Electra (Riverside/Tour); A Family Affair (Cheek by Jowl); When We Are Married (Chichester/West End); The Virgins' Revenge (Soho Poly); Hobson's Choice (West End); Last Resort (Bush); The Seagull, No More Sitting on the Old School Bench (Liverpool); Servant of Two Masters, Schippel, Pythagoras, National Health (Birmingham Rep); Who's Afraid of Virginia Woolf?, Pygmalion, Hindle Wakes, Joking Apart (Scarborough); 'Tis Pity She's A Whore, Ruling the Roost, Three Arrows (Actors' Co). Also RSC seasons in Stratford-upon-Avon and London.

TELEVISION INCLUDES: Little Crackers, All The Small Things, Whatever It Takes, Summerhill, Bad Girls, Doctor Who, Cutting It, Casanova, Poirot, Born and Bred, A Christmas Carol, The Mayor of Casterbridge, Holding On, Making Out, The Pied Piper, Chinese Whispers, The Kitchen Child, Old Men at the Zoo, Miss Marple, Sacred Hearts, Last Day of Summer, The Young Visitors, Great Expectations, Bergerac, The Naked Civil Servant.

FILM INCLUDES: Charlie and the Chocolate Factory, Valiant, Mother's Milk, Legacy, Three and Out, Almost Adult, The Kovak Box, The Knickerman, Honest, Little Voice, Twentyfour Seven, Hollow Reed, Angels and Insects, Captives, Syrup, Jabberwocky.

RADIO INCLUDES: Poetry Please, Lost Voices, The Way We Live Right Now, Dr Zhivago, The Archers, Elizabethan Beauty Law, Shopping for Happiness, Diary of a Nobody, Zdenka, The Pool, Oddbody, Smelling of Roses, The Bridge of San Louis Ray, Les Miserables, Tess of the d'Urbervilles, Twenty Thousand Streets Under The Sky, Return of the Native.

OLLIE BARBIERI (Marcus)

Ollie is making his professional stage debut in Kin.

TELEVISION: Skins.

FILM: Anuvahood.

RADIO: A Small Town Murder.

BUNNY CHRISTIE (Designer)

FOR THE ROYAL COURT: Babies.

OTHER THEATRE INCLUDES: Men Should Weep, Women of Troy, Mrs Affleck, Philistines, The Life of Galileo, Elmina's Kitchen, Dealer's Choice, A Streetcar Named Desire (National); T.S Eliot Festival, After Miss Julie (Donmar); Dance of Death (Royal Dramatic Theatre, Sweden); The Postman Always Rings Twice (WYP/West End); Peter Pan (Dundee Rep); The Prime of Miss Jean Brodie, Mill on the Floss, War and Peace (Shared Experience); Baby Doll (Birmingham Rep/National/West End); The Vagina Monologues (King's Head/Old Vic/West End); Colour of Justice (Tricycle/National/UK tour); The Cosmonaut's Last Message to the Woman He Once Loved in the Soviet Union (Tron, Glasgow).

AWARDS INCLUDE: 2003 Olivier Award for Best Design (A Streetcar Named Desire), Evening Standard Best Design Award (Baby Doll).

FERN DEACON (Nina)

Fern is making her professional stage debut in Kin.

TELEVISION & FILM INCLUDES: Gulliver's Travels, Poirot.

RADIO: Devil in the Fog.

MAYA GERBER (Mimi)

Maya is making her professional stage debut in Kin.

JEREMY HERRIN (Director)

FOR THE ROYAL COURT: Spur of the Moment, Off The Endz, The Priory, Tusk Tusk, The Vertical Hour, That Face (& Duke of York's).

OTHER THEATRE INCLUDES: Marble (Abbey, Dublin); The Family Reunion (Donmar); Blackbird (Market Theatre, Johannesburg); Statement of Regret (National); Sudden Collapses in Public Places, The Boy on the Swing, Gathered Dust and Dead Skin, The Lovers, Our Kind of Fun, Toast, Dirty Nets, Smack Family Robinson, Attachments, From the Underworld, The Last Post, Personal Belongings, ne1, Knives in Hens (Live Theatre).

FOR THE ROYAL COURT, AS ASSISTANT DIRECTOR: My Night with Reg, Babies, Thyestes, The Kitchen.

FILM & TELEVISION INCLUDES: Linked, Dead Terry, Warmth, Cold Calling.

Jeremy is Deputy Artistic Director of the Royal Court.

ELLEN HILL (Nina)

Ellen is making her professional stage debut in Kin.

MIMI KEENE (Janey)

Mimi is making her professional stage debut in Kin.

MADISON LYGO (Janey)

Madison is making her professional stage debut in Kin.

KEVIN McMONAGLE (Mr Thorne)

FOR THE ROYAL COURT: Ladybird, Thyestes, Karate Billy Comes Home, Ambulance.

OTHER THEATRE INCLUDES: Pieces of Vincent, The Unconquered (Arcola); Black Snow, Arturo Ui, Further Than The Furthest Thing (National); Richard III (RSC); Family Reunion (Donmar); Wishbones and Heartthrob (Bush); A Message for the Brokenhearted (Liverpool Playhouse); Russian National Mail (Theatre Doc); Cat & Mouse (Theatre de L'Odeon, Paris); The Miser (Akasaka Playbox); Hamlet and Broken Glass (WYP); Woyzeck, Fall, Girls of Slender Means, Hamlet, Tickly Mince (Edinburgh Festival Fringe); Educating Agnes, Waiting for Godot, The Plough and the Stars, Ghosts (Citizens, Glasgow); Muir, Mcgrotty &Ludmilla, Macbeth, Salvation (Tron, Glasgow).

TELEVISION & FILM INCLUDES: Greenfingers, Rebus, Krakatoa, Quite Ugly One Morning, Monarch of the Glen, Rose and Maloney, Blue Murder, The Immortals, Bramwell, Media Medea, Heartbeat, The Bill, Dr Finlay, Casualty, The Long Roads, Gems, Inspector Morse, Houseman's Tales.

MALCOLM RIPPETH (Lighting Designer)

FOR THE ROYAL COURT: Spur of the Moment.

OTHER THEATRE INCLUDES: Brief Encounter (Kneehigh Theatre/West End/ Broadway); Six Characters in Search of an Author, Calendar Girls (Chichester/West End/UK & Australian tours); The Devil Inside Him (National Theatre Wales); Blast!, King of Prussia, Red Shoes, Don John, Cymbeline, Nights at the Circus, The Bacchae (Kneehigh); The Winslow Boy (also tour), Dumb Show (Rose, Kingston); Dark Side of Buffoon (Coventry/Lyric Hammersmith); His Dark Materials (Birmingham Rep/tour); Edward Gant's Amazing Feats of Loneliness, Faustus (Headlong); Crash, The Grouch, The Lion the Witch and the Wardrobe, Homage to Catalonia (West Yorkshire Playhouse); Mother Courage, Hamlet (English Touring Theatre); James and the Giant Peach (Northampton Royal); The Bloody Chamber, The Little Prince (Northern Stage); Trance (Bush); Confessions of a Justified Sinner, Copenhagen (Edinburgh Royal Lyceum); Monkey! (Dundee Rep); Tutti Frutti (National Theatre of Scotland).

OPERA & DANCE INCLUDES: Armida, Le Nozze Di Figaro, The Philosophers' Stone (Garsington Opera); Carmen Jones (Royal Festival Hall); Seven Deadly Sins (WNO/Diversions Dance) and numerous productions for balletLORENT, most recently Designer Body and Blood, Sweat & Tears.

AWARDS INCLUDE: 2009 Theatregoers' Choice Award for Best Lighting Designer for Brief Encounter and Six Characters in Search of an Author and, as a member of the design team, won the 2010 OBIE Award for Brief Encounter in New York.

CHRISTOPHER SHUTT (Sound Designer)

FOR THE ROYAL COURT: Aunt Dan and Lemon, Arsonists, Free Outgoing, Bliss, Serious Money, Road.

OTHER THEATRE INCLUDES: War Horse (West End/Broadway/National); Nocturnal (Gate); Or You Could Kiss Me, White Guard, Burnt by the Sun, Every Good Boy Deserves Favour, Happy Days (National/World Tour), Coram Boy , Dream Play, Mourning Becomes Electra, Humble Boy, Play Without Words, Albert Speer, Not About Nightingales, Machinal (National); Disappearing Number, Elephant Vanishes, Mnemonic, Street of Crocodiles, Three Lives of Lucie Cabrol (Complicite); All My Sons, Resistible Rise of Arturo Ui (New York); Bacchae, Little Otik (National Theatre of Scotland); Moon for the Misbegotten, All About My Mother (Old Vic); King Lear, Much Ado About Nothing, King John, Romeo & Juliet (RSC); Prince of Homburg, Piaf, The Man Who Had All The Luck (Donmar), Ruined, Judgment Day (Almeida).

RADIO INCLUDES: Shropshire Lad, Maud, After the Quake, Mnemonic, A Disappearing Number.

CIARA SOUTHWOOD (Mimi)

Ciara is making her professional stage debut in Kin.

THE ENGLISH STAGE COMPANY
AT THE ROYAL COURT THEATRE

'For me the theatre is really a religion or way of life. You must decide what you feel the world is about and what you want to say about it, so that everything in the theatre you work in is saying the same thing ... A theatre must have a recognisable attitude. It will have one, whether you like it or not.'

George Devine, first artistic director of the English Stage Company: notes for an unwritten book.

photo: Stephen Cummiskey

As Britain's leading national company dedicated to new work, the Royal Court Theatre produces new plays of the highest quality, working with writers from all backgrounds, and addressing the problems and possibilities of our time.

"The Royal Court has been at the centre of British cultural life for the past 50 years, an engine room for new writing and constantly transforming the theatrical culture." Stephen Daldry

Since its foundation in 1956, the Royal Court has presented premieres by almost every leading contemporary British playwright, from John Osborne's Look Back in Anger to Caryl Churchill's A Number and Tom Stoppard's Rock 'n' Roll. Just some of the other writers to have chosen the Royal Court to premiere their work include Edward Albee, John Arden, Richard Bean, Samuel Beckett, Edward Bond, Leo Butler, Jez Butterworth, Martin Crimp, Ariel Dorfman, Stella Feehily, Christopher Hampton, David Hare, Eugène Ionesco, Ann Jellicoe, Terry Johnson, Sarah Kane, David Mamet, Martin McDonagh, Conor McPherson, Joe Penhall, Lucy Prebble, Mark Ravenhill, Simon Stephens, Wole Soyinka, Polly Stenham, David Storey, Debbie Tucker Green, Arnold Wesker and Roy Williams.

"It is risky to miss a production there." Financial Times

In addition to its full-scale productions, the Royal Court also facilitates international work at a grass roots level, developing exchanges which bring young writers to Britain and sending British writers, actors and directors to work with artists around the world. The research and play development arm of the Royal Court Theatre, The Studio, finds the most exciting and diverse range of new voices in the UK. The Studio runs play-writing groups including the Young Writers Programme, Critical Mass for black, Asian and minority ethnic writers and the biennial Young Writers Festival. For further information, go to www.royalcourttheatre.com/ywp.

"Yes, the Royal Court is on a roll. Yes, Dominic Cooke has just the genius and kick that this venue needs... It's fist-bitingly exciting." Independent

Supported by
**ARTS COUNCIL
ENGLAND**

PROGRAMME SUPPORTERS

The Royal Court (English Stage Company Ltd) receives its principal funding from Arts Council England. It is also supported financially by a wide range of private companies, charitable and public bodies, and earns the remainder of its income from the box office and its own trading activities. The Genesis Foundation supports the Royal Court's work with International Playwrights. Theatre Local is sponsored by Bloomberg. The Jerwood Charitable Foundation supports new plays by new playwrights through the Jerwood New Playwrights series. £10 Monday Nights is sponsored by French Wines: Wines of Quality. The Artistic Director's Chair is supported by a lead grant from The Peter Jay Sharp Foundation, contributing to the activities of the Artistic Director's office. Over the past ten years the BBC has supported the Gerald Chapman Fund for directors.

ROYAL COURT DEVELOPMENT ADVOCATES

John Ayton
Elizabeth Bandeen
Tim Blythe
Anthony Burton
Sindy Caplan
Sarah Chappatte
Cas Donald (Vice Chair)
Allie Esiri
Celeste Fenichel
Anoushka Healy
Emma Marsh (Chair)
Mark Robinson
William Russell
Deborah Shaw Marquardt (Vice Chair)
Nick Wheeler
Daniel Winterfeldt

PUBLIC FUNDING

Arts Council England, London
British Council
European Commission Representation in the UK
New Deal of the Mind

CHARITABLE DONATIONS

American Friends of the Royal Court Theatre
The Brim Foundation*
Gerald Chapman Fund
City Bridge Trust
Columbia Foundation
Cowley Charitable Trust
The Edmond de Rothschild Foundation*
The Epstein Parton Foundation*
Do Well Foundation Ltd*
The Eranda Foundation
Frederick Loewe Foundation*
Genesis Foundation
The Golden Bottle Trust
The Goldsmiths' Company
The H & G de Freitas Charitable Trust
Haberdashers' Company
Jerwood Charitable Foundation
John Thaw Foundation
John Lyon's Charity
J Paul Getty Jnr Charitable Trust
The Laura Pels Foundation*
Leathersellers' Company
Marina Kleinwort Trust
The Martin Bowley Charitable Trust
The Andrew W. Mellon Foundation
Paul Hamlyn Foundation
Jerome Robbins Foundation*
Rose Foundation
Rosenkranz Foundation
Royal Victoria Hall Foundation

The Peter Jay Sharp Foundation*
The Steel Charitable Trust

CORPORATE SUPPORTERS & SPONSORS

BBC
Bloomberg
Coutts & Co
Ecosse Films
French Wines
Grey London
Gymbox
Kudos Film & Television
MAC
Moët & Chandon

BUSINESS ASSOCIATES, MEMBERS & BENEFACTORS

Auerbach & Steele Opticians
Hugo Boss
Lazard
Bank of America Merrill Lynch
Oberon Books
Vanity Fair

INDIVIDUAL MEMBERS

ICE-BREAKERS

Act IV
Anonymous
Rosemary Alexander
Lisa & Andrew Barnett
Ossi & Paul Burger
Mrs Helena Butler
Lindsey Carlon
Mark & Tobey Dichter
Elizabeth & James Downing
Mrs R Jay
Virginia Finegold
Charlotte & Nick Fraser
Mark & Rebecca Goldbart
Alastair & Lynwen Gibbons
Mr & Mrs Green
Sebastian & Rachel Grigg
Mrs Hattrell
Stephen & Candice Hurwitz
David Lanch
Colette & Peter Levy
Yasmine Lever
Watcyn Lewis
Mr & Mrs Peter Lord
David Marks QC
Nicola McFarland
Jonathan & Edward Mills
Ann Norman-Butler
Mrs Georgia Oetker
Janet & Michael Orr
Pauline Pinder
Mr & Mrs William Poeton
The Really Useful Group
Mr & Mrs Tim Reid
Lois Sieff OBE

Nick & Louise Steidl
Laura & Stephen Zimmerman

GROUND-BREAKERS

Alison Davies
Anonymous
Moira Andreae
Nick Archdale
Jane Attias*
Brian Balfour-Oatts
Elizabeth & Adam Bandeen
Ray Barrell
Dr Kate Best
Philip Blackwell
Stan & Val Bond
Mrs D H Brett
Sindy & Jonathan Caplan
Gavin & Lesley Casey
Sarah & Philippe Chappatte
Tim & Caroline Clark
Carole & Neville Conrad
Kay Ellen Consolver
Clyde Cooper
Ian & Caroline Cormack
Mr & Mrs Cross
Andrew & Amanda Cryer
Noel De Keyzer
Rob & Cherry Dickins
Denise & Randolph Dumas
Robyn Durie
Glenn & Phyllida Earle
Margaret Exley CBE
Allie Esiri
Celeste & Peter Fenichel
Margy Fenwick
Tim Fosberry
The Edwin Fox Foundation
John Garfield
Beverley Gee
Mr & Mrs Georgiades
Nick & Julie Gould
Lord & Lady Grabiner
Richard & Marcia Grand*
Nick Gray
Reade & Elizabeth Griffith
Don & Sue Guiney
Jill Hackel & Andrzej Zarzycki
Douglas & Mary Hampson
Sam & Caroline Haubold
Anoushka Healy
Mr & Mrs J Hewett
The David Hyman Charitable Trust
Nicholas Jones
Nicholas Josefowitz
Dr Evi Kaplanis
David P Kaskel & Christopher A Teano
Vincent & Amanda Keaveny
Peter & Maria Kellner*
Steve Kingshott
Mrs Joan Kingsley & Mr Philip Kingsley
Mr & Mrs Pawel Kisielewski
Larry & Peggy Levy
Daisy & Richard Littler

Kathryn Ludlow
David & Elizabeth Miles
Barbara Minto
The North Street Trust
Ann & Gavin Neath CBE
Murray North
Clive & Annie Norton
William Plapinger & Cassie Murray*
Andrea & Hilary Ponti
Wendy & Philip Press
Serena Prest
Julie Ritter
Paul & Gill Robinson
Mark & Tricia Robinson
Paul & Jill Ruddock
William & Hilary Russell
Julie & Bill Ryan
Sally & Anthony Salz
Bhags Sharma
The Michael & Melanie Sherwood Foundation
Tom Siebens & Mimi Parsons
Anthony Simpson & Susan Boster
Brian D Smith
Samantha & Darren Smith
Sheila Steinberg
The Ulrich Family
The Ury Trust
Edgar & Judith Wallner
Mr & Mrs Nick Wheeler
Sian & Matthew Westerman
Lady Carol Woolton
Katherine & Michael Yates*

BOUNDARY-BREAKERS

Katie Bradford
Lydia & Manfred Gorvy
Ms Alex Joffe
Emma Marsh

MOVER-SHAKERS

Anonymous
John and Annoushka Ayton
Cas & Philip Donald
Lloyd & Sarah Dorfman
Duncan Matthews QC
The David & Elaine Potter Foundation
Ian & Carol Sellars
Jan & Michael Topham

HISTORY-MAKERS

Eric Abraham & Sigrid Rausing
Miles Morland

MAJOR DONORS

Rob & Siri Cope
Daniel & Joanna Friel
Jack & Linda Keenan*
Deborah & Stephen Marquardt
Lady Sainsbury of Turville
NoraLee & Jon Sedmak*
The Williams Charitable Trust

*Supporters of the American Friends of the Royal Court (AFRCT)

FOR THE ROYAL COURT

Royal Court Theatre, Sloane Square, London SW1W 8AS
Tel: 020 7565 5050 Fax: 020 7565 5001
info@royalcourttheatre.com, www.royalcourttheatre.com

Artistic Director **Dominic Cooke**
Deputy Artistic Director **Jeremy Herrin**
Associate Director **Sacha Wares***
Artistic Associate **Emily McLaughlin***
Diversity Associate **Ola Animashawun***
Education Associate **Lynne Gagliano***
Producer **Vanessa Stone***
Trainee Director **Monique Sterling**‡
PA to the Artistic Director **David Nock**

Literary Manager **Christopher Campbell**
Senior Reader **Nicola Wass****
Literary Assistant **Marcelo Dos Santos**
Studio Administrator **Clare McQuillan**
Writers' Tutor **Leo Butler***
Pearson Playwright (The John Mortimer Award)
Alia Bano

Associate Director International **Elyse Dodgson**
International Projects Manager **Chris James**
International Assistant **William Drew**

Casting Director (Maternity Cover) **Julia Horan**
Casting Director **Amy Ball**
Casting Assistant **Lotte Hines**

Head of Production **Paul Handley**
JTU Production Manager **Tariq Rifaat**
Production Administrator **Sarah Davies**
Head of Lighting **Matt Drury**
Lighting Deputy **Stephen Andrews**
Listing Assistants **Katie Pitt, Jack Williams**
Lighting Board Operator **Jack Champion**
Head of Stage **Steven Stickler**
Stage Chargehand **Lee Crimmen**
Chargehand Carpenter **Richard Martin**
Building & Productions Assistant **Jerome Jones**
Head of Sound **David McSeveney**
Sound Deputy **Alex Caplen**
Sound Operator **Helen Skiera**
Head of Costume **Iona Kenrick**
Costume Deputy **Jackie Orton**
Wardrobe Assistant **Pam Anson**

Executive Director **Kate Horton**
Head of Finance & Administration **Helen Perryer**
Planning Administrator **Davina Shah**
Senior Finance & Administration Officer
Martin Wheeler
Finance Officer **Rachel Harrison***
Finance & Administration Assistant **Tessa Rivers**
PA to the Executive Director **Holly Handel**

Head of Communications **Kym Bartlett**
Marketing Manager **Becky Wootton**
Press & Public Relations Officer **Anna Evans**
Communications Assistant **Ruth Hawkins**
Communications General Assistants
Kimberley Maloney, James McPhun
Sales Manager **Kevin West**
Deputy Sales Manager **Daniel Alicandro***
Box Office Sales Assistants **Cheryl Gallacher,
Ciara O'Toole, Helen Murray***, **Amanda
Wilkin***, **Stephen Laughton***, **Katherine Clisby***

Head of Development **Gaby Styles**
Senior Development Manager **Hannah Clifford**
Trusts & Foundations Manager **Khalila Hassouna**
Development Manager (Maternity Cover)
Lucy Buxton
Development Assistant **Penny Saward**
US Fundraising Counsel **Tim Runion**
General Fundraising Assistant **Beejal Pandya**

Theatre Manager **Bobbie Stokes**
Deputy Theatre Manager **Daniel O'Neill**
Duty Managers **Fiona Clift***, **Claire Simpson***
Events Manager **Joanna Ostrom**
Bar & Food Manager **Sami Rifaat**
Bar & Food Supervisors **Ali Christian,
Becca Walton**
Head Chef **Charlie Brookman**
Bookshop Manager **Simon David**
Assistant Bookshop Manager **Edin Suljic***
Bookshop Assistant **Vanessa Hammick** *
Customer Service Assistant **Deirdre Lennon***
Stage Door/Reception **Simon David***, **Paul
Lovegrove, Tyrone Lucas**

Thanks to all of our ushers and bar staff.
** The post of Senior Reader is supported by NoraLee & Jon
Sedmak through the American Friends of the Royal Court Theatre.
‡The post of the Trainee Director is supported by the BBC
writersroom.
* Part Time

ENGLISH STAGE COMPANY

President
Dame Joan Plowright CBE

Honorary Council
Sir Richard Eyre CBE
Alan Grieve CBE
Martin Paisner CBE

Council
Chairman **Anthony Burton**
Vice Chairman **Graham Devlin CBE**

Members
Jennette Arnold OBE
Judy Daish
Sir David Green KCMG
Joyce Hytner OBE
Stephen Jeffreys
Wasfi Kani OBE
Phyllida Lloyd CBE
James Midgley
Sophie Okonedo OBE
Alan Rickman
Anita Scott
Katharine Viner
Stewart Wood

E. V. Crowe

Kin

faber and faber

First published in 2010
by Faber and Faber Limited
74–77 Great Russell Street, London WC1B 3DA

Typeset by Country Setting, Kingsdown, Kent CT14 8ES
Printed in England by CPI Bookmarque, Croyon, Surrey

A CIP record for this book
is available from the British Library

ISBN 978-0-571-27216-7

2 4 6 8 10 9 7 5 3 1

For my parents. And my sisters.

Acknowledgements

This play was written during the Royal Court Young Writers Super Group 2009, led by Leo Butler. I would like to thank Leo, all of the writers who commented on the play and the actors who performed in the reading. I would also like to thank Dominic Cooke and everyone at the Royal Court, especially Ruth Little and Jeremy Herrin.

My unending gratitude goes to Giles Smart, Tamzin Robertson, Shiv Malik, Foad Dizadji-Bhamani, Megan Walsh, Serina McDuff, Julian Filer, Cara McCloughlin, Lee McKarkiel, Penelope Skinner, Amy Hodge, Frances Cooke, Kayte Rath, Malcolm Campbell, Joe Harbot, Ruth Fitzsimmons, Lizzie Creer, Zubia Masood, Matt Britton, Peter De Jersey.

Characters

Mimi
ten

Janey
ten

Nina
eleven

Mrs B
forties

Mr Thorne
fifties

Marcus
nineteen

KIN

Two bunk-beds.
    Downstairs, a phone rings out on a loop.

Janey You're not invited though.

    Mimi flips off one bunk and climbs the other.
    She lets her arm hang down.

Mimi It's *in* Austen.

Janey So?

Mimi I'm in Austen.

Janey So?

Mimi I'll be here.

Janey You'll be here, but you won't be *in*.

Mimi You're being a dick.

    Mimi withdraws her arm, lets it hang down again.
    Janey uses it to wrench her off the top bunk onto
    the floor.
    Mimi takes a tennis ball and a tennis racket out of
    Janey's blue box and bats it out of the open window.

I did a midnight feast last term.

Janey You didn't, fuckwad.

    Silence.

Do you mean the time with the toothpaste?

Mimi Ex-fuckeroo-sactly.

Janey You only had laces though.

Mimi Fizzy fucking strawberry dick laces.

Janey And Nags got toothpaste on her arse.

Mimi See.

Silence.

Janey I saw the list.

Mimi Where?

Janey Main board.

Mimi I didn't think they'd put it on the main board.

Janey Main board.

Mimi Tell me.

Janey Look yourself, lazy shit.

Pause.

Mimi I'm not going all the way over to main board. Just tell me.

Janey You can look at supper.

Mimi I'm not going to supper.

Janey You on 'annie'?

Mimi . . .

Janey Just cos Pips came back annie, you're all like, I want to be annie now.

Mimi She went back to Dubai. They had a pool all of August. Did you know that? She looks better annie. I can see all her ribs.

Janey How many are you supposed to have?

Mimi It doesn't matter. As long as it's the same on both sides.

Janey You'll be able to count when she goes up for cutlery. She's stopped wearing a bra.

Pause.

Mimi No, I'm not going to supper.

Janey I don't have to go annie.

Mimi We know.

Janey I eat whatever.

Mimi You ate my tuck.

Janey Fuck off, you had your tuck, all, first day back.

Pause.

Mimi I'll go to rec swim, then come back here.

Janey I'll sneak you a banana.

Mimi I don't want a banana.

Janey I got a big jumper for it.

Mimi They'll make you change it. Like your skirt.

Janey *I* stopped rolling up my skirt. I got it cut off at the bottom, which is cooler and my mum's friend did it herself so they can fuck off when they find out.

Mimi I saw at the post table –

Janey I never check the post table.

Mimi – Mrs B, bollocking you.

Janey I'll tell Grunter the banana's for you when she catches me. Then they'll ask why and I'll say Mimi's gone annie, and then they'll make you come to lunch, eat cottage cheese, pass out at the tray stack and send you home.

Mimi They just love you if you go annie anyway. It's only people who do art who go really annie. I can't draw!

Pause.

What am I then?

Janey Go and see main board.

Mimi Just tell me.

Janey You didn't tell me when I got made wing attack.

Mimi Cos I was fucking centre, and I knew you'd have an epi.

Janey Everyone saw it on main board.

Mimi I'm sorry I didn't tell you about wing attack. But this is different.

Janey No.

Mimi You don't even do drama.

Janey Maybe cos *you're* in it.

Mimi What am I?

Janey I don't even know why they're doing the dog shit one. They should do the school one again.

Mimi What one?

Janey The posh one.

Mimi *Prime of Miss Jean Brodie*?

Janey Yah. That one's got all parts for everyone.

Mimi They do it all the time. And it's shit lines. And it's like saying here is like *Malory Towers*. It's shit.

Janey *Crème de la crème.*

Mimi I don't understand you.

Janey *Crème de la crème*. First line – first thing she says is, 'You girls, my girls, are the *crème de la crème*.'

Mimi I don't remember.

Janey It means they're going to rule the world.

Mimi I don't remember.

Janey Cos you were obsessed with Annabelle Phillips. First fucking line, remember?!

Mimi What? Fuck off.

Janey You were like, why can't we do *Jesus Christ Superstar* again because I want to fucking marry Annabelle Phillips. You were fucking all over Jesus, in love with Jesus and Annabelle.

Mimi She looked like a man.

Janey I told you! I knew it. I'm going to tell her. She takes our prep.

Mimi Please don't, Janey. Don't.

Janey If they'd done that one I'd tell you you're Miss Brodie. Best of the best. But they chose a shit play. Grunter loves me, I won't even have to hide the banana. She'll let me take it out.

Mimi What am I?

Janey If you go and knock on Mr Edwards's door and tell him you want him to rape you, I'll tell you.

Mimi Not right now.

Janey Tell him you saw the flasher and you don't want to be a virgin and that you want to do position of the fortnight out of *More* magazine and that you want him to rape you.

Mimi I've got him for CDT.

Janey So? He would if you wanted. And you already know how to use the jigsaw, so you've got nothing to lose.

Mimi I still don't fully understand . . . I don't understand hydraulics, actually. Fucking tell me, fuckshit.

Janey It's nearer to go to Mr Edwards's than to go down to main board. He already knows you fancy him.

Mimi I don't fancy him.

Janey No, because you fancy Annabelle Phillips and you want her to touch you.

> *Silence.*

Give me your tuck-box key and I'll tell you.

Mimi I don't have any tuck in there.

Janey You do.

Mimi I don't.

Janey You won dorm prize last week and I saw you put your Mars bar in there. And I know you haven't had it yet.

Mimi I'm saving it. For chapel on Sunday. Get me through it.

Janey And you owe me ten p. Give me the key, ten p, and I'll tell you.

> *Silence.*
> *Janey points at Mimi's blue box, and won't relax her arm until Mimi moves.*
> *Mimi goes to her blue box where she keeps everything she owns and scrabbles around.*

Mimi Janey . . .

Janey Proctor!

Silence.

You don't know who Proctor is.

Mimi smiles, goes and gets a book out of her box. She starts leafing through.

Mimi You better not be shitting me because Proctor is on every page.

Janey And he fucks everyone in the play.

Mimi Does he?

Janey Yah! He fucks the twelve-year-old who tricks him and he fucks his wife and he fucks some other kid in the jury during the trial. And Mrs Parsons always makes you do the stage directions, so basically you're going to have to fuck everyone in our class.

Mimi No I won't.

Janey You will see.

Mimi He's like, about being strong and doing the right thing. He's Marky Mark. Or that other actor.

Janey He's not.

Mimi I saw the film.

Janey Itchy chin. It's a fifteen.

Mimi Anna Martins sneaked it.

Janey Meh.

Mimi He's the good one. He's like, 'fuck you' and strong. In the story . . . in the story –

Janey You tell stories the shit way.

Mimi In the story –

Janey 'And then, no! Wait, before. Then!' – Dickwad!

Mimi Shussssh!

Janey 'Before, then, no! Before, then . . .'

Mimi Proctor has an affair with a blonde girl . . .

Janey Then.

Mimi I'm telling it! All the other girls say they can see devils.

Janey Before.

Mimi Shut uuuup! Before that he's pissed off with his wife, then his wife says it's all her fault, before that the know-it-alls try to tell everyone what to do in the town, then something bad happens to Proctor, before his wife lies to protect him.

Janey Then –

Mimi Shut uuuuup! Then everyone feels bad. Before that even in the story, you're like, 'Yeah, whatever,' about all of it because Proctor is like, 'Whatever, fuck you, I'm Proctor.' And you want to clap him or something because he's so fucking nails. Something-like-that.

Janey Just so you know, doing drama doesn't make you popular.

Pause.

Mimi What is it tonight?

Janey Freezer Surprise.

Mimi What's the surprise?

Janey I can smell cutlets.

Mimi Vom.

Janey OK. Make sure you piss in the pool. See you after.

18

*Neither of them moves. A bell goes. Feet on the floor
above thunder about.*

Mimi Who do you think the cleverest teacher in our
school is?

Janey Mrs King.

Mimi Why?

Janey She worked for Intelligence.

Mimi But now she teaches geography.

Janey Just cos you're not doing geography this term you
think anyone doing it is dumb-arse.

Mimi Mmm.

Janey You think you're it.

Mimi Mmm. I don't. I swear.

Janey They only want you to be Proctor cos you're gay
and they know you wanted to fuck Jesus.

Silence.

I'll tell her to invite you after whispers. I'll tell her you're
my best friend.

Mimi It's OK.

Janey You are my best friend. You have to be actually.
They think you mean I get good marks.

Pause.

Mimi I'll be asleep.

Janey You won't be.

Mimi Who says?

Janey Me.

Pause. Mimi looks at the back of the book.

Mimi I just read the end. I was right.

Janey Does he die?

Mimi They kill him.

Janey How?

Mimi They take his name.

Janey That's stupid.

Mimi They don't let him be Proctor any more.

Janey That's stupid.

Mimi And then they kill him.

Janey *How?*

Mimi They hang him.

Pause.

Janey Why?

Mimi They hang him.

Janey Why?

Mimi He knows they're all fuckers.

*They both run suddenly to Mimi's tuck box. They
fight over it on the floor. Mimi kicks Janey and picks
up the tuck box. She throws it out of the window.
   They go back to their bunks and lie there, bricking it.
Silence.
   Mrs B comes into the room.
   She stands for a moment and looks at the dorm.*

Mrs B Five points off.

*She lets a tennis ball roll out of her hand on to the floor.
   They wait.*

Janey How long was she there?

Mimi Fuck knows.

Janey She heard you swear.

Mimi Better me than you.

Janey My parents won't see me at Christmas if she tells them one more bad thing.

Mimi It was me.

   Silence.

Janey At least she didn't hear me say – (*shouting*) Mr B's a fat fuck!

   Janey laughs.

Lights out, whispers, then I'll come and get you.

   Pause.

Mimi Don't.

BEFORE

Mrs B on a chair.
   On the phone.
   Eating an orange.

Mrs B You should come down here, Headmistress.
   You should come and see for yourself.
   It's an impossible bracket to supervise. They are like dogs. The winter term is always a bad term for the girls. Except for Christmas and the birth of Jesus.
   Yes.
   They are like ferrets. You know what I mean, Headmistress.
   I'm going to put it in my report.
   I know the Junior School Report.

That is the tradition, yes.

Everybody expects the report to say they are a delight. They are very bright. They are pure as light.

But they are small dogs, Headmistress. I must report what I see. They are small dogs in packs or pairs, doing what small dogs do.

More than barking. Worse than barking.

If something happens I will have no choice but to explain it. If something tragic happens I will have to explain it. I will have to call it something.

No. It is not that. It is not bullying. Dogs do not bully. You don't understand the situation. I will put it all in my report. I am in a process of investigation.

I understand them, Headmistress. I do. I see them.

A tennis ball lands on her head.

They are growling, Headmistress. I must go.

One more thing. I've given it a title. *Erziehungsroman.* I'm going to call it that long German word.

It means a Roman Education.

I could say it in English, yes. But I think it gives it more punch in German.

Yes, it's just the title of the report I'm working on. Instead of calling it Junior School Report. I just thought it was a nice idea.

You have to go?

She hangs up.
She stands up. Her head hurts.
She picks up the ball.
A tuck box smashes onto the chair where she was sitting.
Deodorant, photos, books and papers, a teddy, a toy troll, a Mars bar and a lock-with-a-key diary, all roll out.
Mrs B takes the diary, wipes her hands of the orange and has a bite of the Mars bar.

By the card phone.
  Nina on the phone.
  Mimi presses her face up to the phone.
  She sits down cross-legged.
  Nina hangs up. Drops the phone off the hook.
  Mimi dials.

Mimi Hi Daddy, can I speak to Mummy?

Pause.

Hi Mummy. I've been queuing for two hours. I actually have. Can you call me back?

She hangs up. It rings right away. Mimi winces.

Hello?

Pause.

I'll see if I can find her.

Mimi looks for 'Alice'. She walks loudly up and down, slams a door twice.

I'm sorry I can't find her.

Pause.

She's not in the Com. Common room. I checked. Or her dorm.

Pause.

Bye.

Mimi slumps.
  The phone rings. Mimi doesn't move.
  Nina walks past, looks at the phone, doesn't answer it.
  Janey comes in, picks up the phone.

Don't pick up!

Janey smiles and moves like a dutiful maid.

Janey Hello?
It's for Nina.

Mimi She just got off the phone.

Janey Her parents are fucking divorced. Don't shit on her cos of that. Is she only supposed to speak to one of them?
It's her dad that pays the dicking fees.
(*On the phone.*) Hang on while I find her Mr Thorpe-Cunthorpe.

Janey goes.
She comes back with Nina.

Mimi My mum's trying to get through, please don't be long, Nins.

Nina Thanks, wallybrain.

Mimi Seriously, you can have my pudding next time it's apricot cobblers.

Nina You didn't invite me to eat your birthday cake.

Mimi That was a mistake.

Nina Maybe.
Hi, Daddy.
I just spoke to Mummy. What's Hong Kong like?

Pause.

OK.

She hangs up.

He had a business call.

Mimi Bad luck.

Nina Thanks for getting me, Janey.

Janey I still hate your guts. I did it to piss Mimi off.

The phone rings. Nina leaves.
Janey passes the phone to Mimi. She gets up and takes it.

I'm next.

Mimi puts her hand over the speaker part.

Mimi Ange is next.

Janey Says who?

Mimi Her torch is here.

Janey You can't queue like that. You have to be here. I'll wait.

Mimi I'll save your place.

Janey Ange'll cry shitwipes.

Mimi OK, but the queue starts further back.

Janey I have to be in front of the torch, dipshit.

She sits right next to Mimi's feet.

Mimi (*on the phone*) Hello?
Just calling to say hi. I don't have anything to talk about really.
I'm OK.
They're really hard. I've been revising loads and loads.
I know I got 91 in maths.
Yeah.
How's Daddy?
That sounds funny.
School on Saturday, then I had to play a match. Took us three hours on the coach, then . . . yes, it was very cold. I slept on the way back. We didn't win. I don't know. Mrs H said our defence was a bit less good than usual. Nicole is still in Nigeria, in her head. She moves

too slowly. I think the chinks and the black girls can be really lazy. Then we had supper then we watched a video. No, one of the old ones we have. We watched *Casualty* first actually. And then today we had chapel. One of those people who do the boxes where you can't see it until it spells out 'TRUTH' or 'HOPE' or something. We were asked to think about what kind of person we want to be. Who we expected to become. And about going to heaven.

There wasn't much left by the time I got to lunch. Some bread. Then I just wondered around until supper. Around the grounds. I went up to see if I could take Mrs Walker's dog out but she wasn't there. I mean, I could hear her inside, but she wasn't opening the door. And I got stung by a bee.

The nurse doesn't work Sundays.

No, they said there's nothing you can put on bee stings.

Mummy – there's nothing you can put on them. They're right. It doesn't even hurt very much now.

And now we have early bed before Monday. I have to do my sheets.

It's OK. I'm OK.

She starts crying.

(*Crying.*) No I'm not . . .

Tears are rolling down her face.

Nooooo.

Tell me about Jaffa.

Did he?! Silly dog.

If you want to ask me things you have to make it so I can say yes or no.

Yes.

Yes.

Yes.

Don't say that! I don't mean to make you upset. I'm not, Mummy.

I am doing my best. I promise. I know I'll see you at the end of term. The play, tests, carol service.

Janey's fine. She's OK. Her parents can't come to the end-of-term carol service either.

Janey Tell her hi.

Mimi Janey says hi.

Janey Tell her to send me some fizzy laces.

Mimi She didn't say anything. Mummy, you have to ask me yes or no. I can't say.

Not those kinds of questions. Ask me other questions. Mummy, please . . .

Please . . .

No, it's OK. Don't worry. There's a really big queue for the phone and I have to do my bed sheets tonight.

Please can you send me some tights. Black.

I love you tons and masses too. Really tons and tons and tons.

I'm OK.

Love you, bye, bye, bye, bye . . .

Janey gets up and clicks down the receiver lever.
The phone rings.
Janey screams with frustration.

Janey Hello? She's gone to bed. I'm a million per cent positive. We literally just checked for Nish two minutes ago. She was asleep. Do you want me to wake her up?

Bye.

Tell Ange there won't be time for her to call out before lights out. Take her torch.

I mean *take* her torch. I hope it's not my dad.

Mimi Why?

Janey I told you why.

Janey dials, fast fast.

27

Oh, hi, Dad, is Mum there?
It's OK. Can you tell her to call me?

Mimi starts walking away.

Don't worry.

Mute both ends.

Dad? OK, bye.

Janey hangs up, looks for Mimi, who is gone.

THEN

Janey and Mimi are waiting on the step with tennis rackets. It is colder and darker than before.

Janey I never see you now.

Mimi You do.

Janey 'The play, the play, the play.'

Mimi Sorry.

Nina walks outside carrying letters.

Janey It's your fuckbuddy.

Mimi Hi, Nina.

Janey Don't you two fuck in the play?

Nina What are you doing?

Mimi We were playing tennis against the wall but now we're waiting to be bollocked.

Nina Mrs B is in a staff meeting.

Mimi Till when?

Nina Fuck knows. Before prep?

Mimi We could leave a note?

Janey Way you look at her means you fancy her.

Nina I've got to post the letters.

Janey Do you like the play?

Nina It's really long.

Janey Do you have to kiss Mimi?

Nina . . .

Janey Oh my fucking god, oh my fuckeroo.

Nina Someone is coming to watch it.

Mimi Who?

Nina One of the governors.

Janey watches them talk.

Mimi Why?

Nina They think outside people should come in sometimes.

Mimi Why?

Nina To give a prize?

Mimi Tuck vouchers?

Nina Like a book.

Mimi I've got fuckloads of books.

Nina So.

Mimi So I've got enough bits of paper fucked together.

Nina Do you like the play and Mrs Eccle?

Mimi She's cool.

Nina What do you like about it?

Janey puts her elbow on Mimi's shoulder.

Janey Fucking you.

Mimi I like the boots I get to wear and that Proctor gets to shout a lot. He's sort of good and bad at the same time.

Nina What's your worst line?

Mimi 'I want my life!' Someone else says something, then I say, 'I will have my life' – something, something – 'You will not use me, it is not part of salvation that you should use me!' It's a bit knobby.

Janey Then you two have sex.

Mimi 'Because it is my name! Because I cannot have another in my life!' 'Leave me my name!'

Janey Dogshit lines.

Nina I think you're good.

Janey At 69-ers. Mimi's also fucking Mr –

Nina Everyone is.

Janey gets up, annoyed.

Janey Can you do a handstand?

Nina Yes.

Janey Go on.

Nina It's wet and there's glass.

Janey You can use the wall.

Nina That's where all the glass is.

Janey Mimi just did one.

Nina Did you?

Mimi doesn't move.

Janey Give me the letters.

Janey takes the letters. Nina does a handstand against the wall.

Hold it. Hold. It . . .!

Janey claps.
   Nina comes down and smiles.

Now take your knickers off.

Nina doesn't move.

I took mine off.

They sit in silence.
   Nina takes her knickers off and leaves them on the floor with her feet.

Now do a handstand.
   Now do a handstand.

Nina does a handstand.

Hold it, hold it . . .

Janey puts the racket next to her. She pulls Mimi to walk away slowly. Janey takes the letters.

BEFORE

Janey hits a tennis ball against a wall.

Janey Did you dorm vote?

Mimi Yes.

Janey Did you put me? I put you.

Mimi Yeah.

Janey You put me down.

Mimi Janey. Yeah.

Janey Swear it? In the vote box?

Mimi Hope to die.

Pause.

It's my turn.

Janey What did she say, dickwad? Headmistress . . .

Silence.

Mimi Asked me what I wanted to be.

Janey I said vet.

Mimi I want to be a vet! That's my thing!

Janey She'll think you copied me.

Mimi That's my thing. I wanted to be a vet, we can't both be vets. I can't believe you did that.

Janey What else?

Mimi She said about the scholarship.

Janey The suck-up prize.

Mimi She said it would depend on my performance this term.

Janey The suck-up prize depends on how much arse-licking you sucky-suck suck up. If your tongue makes it right up to the hairy part.

Mimi Urgh!

Janey If you really liked biology, you'd know what I'm talking about.

Pause.

This is the only good wall in the place.

Mimi The rest are neo-gothic.

Janey This is the only redbrick, worth-a-shit wall in the place.

Mimi This is the cheap wall.

Janey It's the only wall where the ball doesn't bounce back at you funny.

Mimi This is the shit new wall. This is where they ran out of limestone.

Janey I suppose that makes me common?

Pause.

And what else?

Mimi That's it.

Janey Did she say she thought you could be a vet?

Mimi She didn't say.

Janey Did you shit yourself?

Mimi Yes.

Janey Show me.

Mimi laughs.

I said 'consisted of'.

Mimi That was my new word!

Janey I said my ambitions 'consisted of becoming a vet or a barrister'.

Mimi That was my new word.

Janey She said that I consisted of a fine ambition for someone about to move into main school.

Mimi Janey . . .

Janey She'll probably tell your parents you copied me wanting to be a vet. And then they'll know. And they'll hate your guts.

Mimi My parents don't hate me. I said it was because I love animals. Which makes sense, and she can tell I love them. I want to work with animals.

Janey You're not allowed to help *all* of them. Some of them are OK to just die in pain.

Janey continues to hit the ball.

Mimi What did you say?

Janey I said because I love maths, chemistry and biology. And my uncle is a vet and I help him during the school holidays.

Mimi Your uncles are all bankers. Isn't your dad actually a vet?

Janey So?

Pause.

Mimi My turn.

Janey Are you sick yet?

Mimi No. You?

Janey Take your scarf off.

Mimi takes it off.

Mimi Three down.

Janey It's not enough to call off the carol service.

Mimi I know.

Janey Can't you make whole of Austen get sick?

Mimi How?

Janey Spread the sick.

Mimi We're sharing with three psychos who never get sick. One is sick.

Janey Not enough.

Mimi They want people to get better so they don't have to look after them in san.

Janey You die in san anyway.

Mimi Nurse Ellie sits on your face to suffocate you.

Janey Lisa Charman came out of san annie.

Mimi That's true.

Janey If there's one thing that I hate more in this shit place it's the carol service. It's the most boring piece of shit lesson we ever have and it's the same shit every year with the tree and the lights and Mrs Ambercroft telling us to 'project our voices' even though there's a microphone and the 'this is the word' and 'verse one chapter seven' fucking funny letters and waking up and dickhead Samantha singing the solo 'Once in Royal David' and I can't stay awake and we have to do it three times. When is ever fucking Christmas three times? I don't work for Christmas. You can work for Christmas. You would be Christmas slave. If you take your shoes off you'll get sick faster. It's fucking freezing.

Mimi I'm not taking my DMs off.

Pause.

Janey Your turn.

Mimi stands up to take the racket.

Two more hits, hang on.

Janey hits the ball hard, it smashes a window and doesn't come back. The glass shatters by the wall.

That was on your go.

THEN

Mr Thorne uses the urinal.
  Mimi dressed as Proctor comes out of the cubicle.
  Mr Thorne zips up.
  Mimi takes her hat off.

Mimi It's normally empty in here.

  Pause.

Sorry.

  Pause.

Mr Thorne You're doing very well.

Mimi I'm not.

Mr Thorne You've remembered all your lines.

Mimi Not a hundred per cent.

Mr Thorne I don't think he'll mind.

Mimi Who?

Mr Thorne Miller.

Mimi Who's that?

Mr Thorne The writer.

Mimi I know who Arthur Miller is.

Mr Thorne . . .

Mimi Isn't he dead?

Mr Thorne No.

Mimi Oh.

Pause.

Mr Thorne It really depends if you're adding in or taking away.

Mimi I've missed loads out.

Pause.

Mr Thorne What about the next half?

He looks at his watch.

I'm due to collect my daughter.

Mimi From where?

Mr Thorne My wife.

Mimi Why?

Mr Thorne She lives with me every other Saturday.

Pause.

The Headmistress mentioned you a bit. I think.

Mimi Did she?

Mr Thorne I think it was you.

Mimi Does she think I'm head-girl material?

Mr Thorne I think she thinks, you're . . . I don't know.

Mimi You can tell.

Mr Thorne Can you?

Mimi Can't you?

Mr Thorne You're only ten.

Mimi I won't change.

Mr Thorne washes his hands.

Excuse me, what does a governor do?

Mr Thorne I advise, donate, donate my wisdom.

Mimi What do you say?

Mr Thorne I'm not actually asked very often.

Mimi Oh.

Mr Thorne I say to carry on! Of course the school does a very good job with all its little people. Carry on! Carry on!

Pause.

Get on with it.

Mimi Is this a good school?

Mr Thorne Yes. I think so.

Mimi Does your daughter come here?

Mr Thorne No.

Mimi Why is it a good school?

Mr Thorne I don't think schools should be too overly accountable. You're responsible for you, Sir.

Pause.

We should head in . . .

He opens the door.
Mimi adjusts her hat in the mirror.

You do look like him.

Mr Thorne notices Mimi is reluctant to leave. He finds his wine glass on the side.

Do you want me to find you a friend?

Mimi She's not coming. We had a fight.

Mr Thorne You had a fight with your wife?

Mimi My friend.

Mr Thorne Was it a big fight?

Mimi Yeah.

Mr Thorne What did you fight about?

Mimi Our future.

Mr Thorne Sorry.

Mimi It's private.

   Pause.

Mr Thorne Are your parents here?

Mimi No. They're moving to France. Germany. France. France.

Mr Thorne How lovely! But also *quel dommage* for you I suppose.

Mimi *Oui.*

Mr Thorne France is a very long way from your community in Salem. But maybe after the trial you can visit them.

   Pause.

Mimi I won't get to go home at exeats, only main holidays. And it will be harder to phone. I've been trying to speak to them for weeks. They haven't replied.

Mr Thorne Both of them?

Mimi Mummy and Daddy.

Pause.

Mr Thorne They'll actually be wondering where you are backstage.

Mimi I don't mind.

Mr Thorne What will people think of you?

Mimi They'll think: 'Where is she?'

Mr Thorne People will start to imagine you are hiding. That you are hiding here. You should nip off to backstage.

Mimi It's not really backstage, it's a classroom. It's usually called D4.

Pause.

In about a week, all the wasps will come in here to die. They fly into the last loo, and conk out on the floor. I watch them.

Mr Thorne You shouldn't come here then.

Mimi They come in here with a sting, and then they conk out. I tell everyone every year. It always happens anyway.

Mr Thorne Careful. *Bee* careful.

Mimi Thank you, Mr Thorne.

Mr Thorne smiles.

Am I going to get the prize?

Mr Thorne What prize?

Mimi The best performer prize?

Mr Thorne Oh, no, dear.

Mimi Why not?

Mr Thorne I can't remember what we said. You can come off a bit. You were excellent.

Pause.

A bit dramatic.

Mimi Are you an expert?

Mr Thorne I am not a performance expert.

Mimi You're not an expert?

Mr Thorne I come to see the little people.

Mimi Are you a paedophile?

Mr Thorne No.

Mimi OK.

Mr Thorne I have a daughter.

Mimi I understand.

Mr Thorne It's interesting to see all of you. Still in the grip of nature, doing as you please, beneath the word of the law, beyond reproach from God.

Mimi What do you mean?

Mr Thorne I suppose I mean you can't do anything wrong. You're too young!

Mimi I'm ten.

Mr Thorne Oh, ten.

Mimi What can happen at ten?

Mr Thorne Nothing. You can't go to prison at ten. In this country.

Mimi But you're not an expert?

Mr Thorne I'm a father.

Pause.

Mimi But you're not an expert.

Pause.

Mr Thorne Someone else will definitely get the prize, but really you should enjoy the play for its own sake.

Pause.

Mimi What's the prize, *please*? May I ask.

Mr Thorne Book vouchers.

Mimi Then it really doesn't matter.

Mr Thorne I think you ought to *want* to get the prize.

Mimi I know.

Mr Thorne For your own development.

Mimi I do understand the system.

Mr Thorne The point is always progressional. Where do you, Sir . . . Miss, see yourself in five years' time?

Mimi Lower sixth.

Mr Thorne Lower sixth! I'd love to hear your dreams.

Pause.

Mimi I want to be a vet.

Mr Thorne . . .

Mimi I like animals. Like the wasps. Like Proctor does.

Mr Thorne Don't you want to be a princess?

Mimi No.

Mr Thorne Tell me something else, little person.

Mimi Proctor, Proctor is in 'agriculture'.

Mr Thorne studies her for a moment.

Mr Thorne Have the recent heavy rains been much of a problem for you?

Mimi takes her hat off.

I can hear everyone going back in . . .

Nina bursts through the door dressed as Abigail, in a white bonnet and black smock.

Nina (*noticing Mr Thorne*) Oh, hello, Mr Thorne.

Pause.

Am I going to win the prize?
Mimi, I have to talk to you. Privately.

Mr Thorne Actually, I'm not sure if I should leave you in here with a young girl.

Mr Thorne realises he has made a mistake. He shakes Mimi's hand.

Good luck with the trial. I've had a wonderful time.

He leaves. He comes back in for his glass. Leaves.

Nina Don't hate me.

Mimi What?

Nina Mrs B just found me and asked me. She's writing a report.

Mimi What?

Nina About us unbolting the windows and playing cards in the 'to-the-death' tournament and about other stuff.

Mimi Itchy chin.

Nina I'm telling the truth.

Mimi What did she say?

Nina She asked me if I see anything.

Mimi What did you say?

Nina I do see things.

Mimi What?

Nina You know what I see.

Mimi What do you see?

Nina Other stuff. You know what!

Mimi Are you fucking dicking with me? You dick, you complete dick. You fucking dick, Nina. You're a complete dick, I fucking hate you, you dickhead, you fucking dick. You're such a diiiiiiick.

Nina They'll ask you about it.

Mimi When?

Nina They have to ask you about it. They'll want to do something.

Mimi What are they going to do?

Nina Tell our parents. Or worse.

Mimi They won't tell *them*. They caught Imogen who's head of house with drugs and they didn't tell her parents.

Nina That's because she's so good at lacrosse.

Mimi I'm good at lacrosse.

Nina You lost last week.

Mimi At least I don't get an off-games slip for my fucking period every other week.

Nina You haven't started.

Mrs B comes into the room.

Mrs B The play isn't finished yet. Nina, Mimi . . . out –

Nina Oh, only, Mimi thinks she's started her period.

Mrs B leaves.

Mimi You're going to have to tell them you make stuff up. You do make stuff up. Did you see how she just fucking looked at me? She's psycho.

Nina I know what I see.

Mimi You're such a dick.

Nina Sorry.

Mimi I'm never talking to you again if they crap on me. You're such a dobber. I *knew* you were a dobber. I just fucking knew it. I could tell by the way you do your hair. DICK!

Pause.

What's my line when I go in?

Nina Can't remember.

Mimi You fucker, Nina –

She thinks, desperately.

It's about you as a harlot and my wife as truthful. And all the men are like – you're fucking scum. And when you all get to scream . . . how do I start?

Nina I'm really sorry, Mims. I don't want them to say I have to give up my hamster. (*To appease her.*) You do look really annie round your face.

Mimi Itchy chin.

She looks in the mirror.

But, OK, thanks.

Mimi shrugs.

I didn't do anything wrong.

Nina It's Janey.

Mimi Shut up.

Pause.

Nina Tell on her.

Start-of-the-play music sounds from outside, then a drumbeat.
Mimi goes to leave.

Mimi, what's a harlot?

Mimi Fuck knows.

BEFORE

Janey is reading a pile of letters.
She recognises the handwriting of one.
In the letter is a tape cassette.
An announcement introducing The Crucible *can be heard from the window. Start-of-the-play music, then a slow drumbeat.*
Janey reads aloud.

Dear Mummy and Daddy,
How are you? I am fine, thank you. Thank you for the postcard you sent me with the horse on it. It made me think about the horse I was allowed to use that belonged to the lady near my old school before we moved the time before. But it's not a brown one. I have put it up on my bunk. I snuck down to J5 classroom and borrowed some Blu-tack, as we must have missed it off the kit list.

I wish you were not going to move as soon as you are, again. Will you tell me when you move? Anne Mathers says it is very far away. Is it another country? Maybe you can tell me when we speak on the phone on Sunday. I will try to call you at 7.30 but sometimes Katy Jones cries for a very long time and I get annoyed.

I wanted to talk to you at exeat but we did all of those very fun things like going to the park, and so now I have stayed up late with the torch you gave me. I think it needs new batteries because the light is not very strong. Or if it is the bulb do I get a new torch? If yes, how do I do this? I wanted to write to you because I find it hard to say how much I don't want to be here any more. I can't seem to describe how bad I think this school is. It is hard to say without sounding ungrateful. I try to keep my sheets to smell of when Mummy washed them, but it goes very quickly.

I made you a mix tape of some songs I think explain how I feel. 'Everybody Hurts' by REM. Please listen to the words.

Janey gets up, puts the tape in the tape player and presses play. Listens. Then presses stop.

The other thing is two pleases. Please, please, please, please, please, please can I have a bra to wear because I know some of the other girls are wearing them now, I can tell. And also this is what I think is most important and I can't tell you why but pleeeease please please please can you ask Mrs B not to put me in a dorm with Janey next term. I really really really really don't want to be in a dorm with her! It will mess everything up.

I'm serious. But please don't phone the school. Just say somehow. I'm not sure I can even eat until I know for certain I won't have to room with her next term.

Love to Jaffa, and tonnes and tonnes of love to you. Sorry I spelt tonnes wrong last time. Love, Mimi.

Janey folds up the letter. She hides the letter. She puts the pile in the plastic dorm bin.

She then picks up the bin and we can hear her going through multiple heavy fire doors.

She comes back in covered in black soot, the front of her hair is singed.

She walks around the room.

She jumps up to see if she can touch the ceiling, then the light.

She looks around.

She pulls out her pyjamas from under her pillow, gets into them without revealing herself, in an elaborate transition of clothing.

She neatly folds her clothes on her chair. And climbs into bed.

She gets back out and turns the light off.

Applause for the play can be heard from across the courtyard.

After a while Mimi comes in, turns the light on, Janey sits up, Mimi turns the light off immediately.

In the dark Mimi notices Janey's clothes neatly folded and knows something is wrong.

THEN

In Mrs B's study.
  Mimi is in her stripy dressing gown.
  Mrs B is also in her dressing gown.
  Nina is in her nightie at the wall.
  Mrs B has oven gloves on and a burned-out bin.

Mrs B Do you know what a bully is, Mimi?

Mimi Yes.

Mrs B What's a bully?

Mimi A mean girl. A bully.

Mrs B What do we do with bullies here, Mimi?

Mimi Expel them.

Mrs B We boot them out.

Mimi Yes.

Mrs B Do you know any bullies, Mimi?

Mimi No.

Mrs B Do you know who did this?

Mimi No.

Mrs B I think it was Janey. I think Janey took the letters weeks ago. She waited until a moment came for her to read them quietly, then she burned them.

Mimi No.

Mrs B Plain and simple.

Mimi Are you sure?

Mrs B The Headmistress thinks she is a bully.

Mimi Really?

Mrs B We are both worried that you are being bullied. That you are a victim of some nasty bullying. We are all worried about you. Particularly as it is nearly Christmas.

Mimi No.

Mrs B So why don't you want to be in a dorm with Janey next term?

Mimi I don't know.

Mrs B You wrote 'Anyone except Janey'. You wrote that on your dorm vote piece of card and put it in the dorm vote box outside my office.

Mimi Yes.

Mrs B Did you have an argument?

Mimi Yes.

Mrs B And now you've made up?

Mimi Yes.

Mrs B So now I can put you together?

Mimi I'd prefer to share with Clarey.

Mrs B She's put Alice down and Alice has put her down.
 I'm going to have to put you with Janey. Unless you
can tell me the truth.

Mimi . . .

Mrs B I don't like the word 'bully'.

 Pause.

Really she's your friend.

Mimi Yes.

Mrs B She's your special friend.

Mimi I don't know what you mean.

Mrs B You are together.

Mimi Not always.

Mrs B Together.

Mimi Not for prep.

Mrs B You are together.

Mimi No.

Mrs B You can tell me, Mimi. It's all going in my report.

Mimi Really?

Mrs B I can see marks on your neck and shoulders.

Mimi That's from lacrosse.

Mrs B I can see marks on your cheek.

Mimi No.

Mrs B Someone has scratched 'J' with the end of a compass onto your shoulder blade. And they have kissed you hard. Like a love bite.

Mimi That was me.

Mrs B Not possible.

Mimi It was.

Mrs B Either you are with Janey. That is to say, you have feelings for Janey, butterflies for Janey, or she is a bully. One or the other. We have seen you in your bunks.

  Silence.

And she has hurt you without your consent. She is with you without consent. That means you didn't agree and then that is something else. Did you say yes?

Mimi We play cards in our bunks.

Mrs B Go on.

Mimi Sorry, Mrs B. I don't understand. Do you want me to explain the cards? It's 'snatch and grab' or sometimes we play sardines. When you have to hide together. Maybe you saw us hide together.

Mrs B Interesting. Mimi, you know I'm very experienced. I'm an expert in children.

Mimi . . . Yes.

Mrs B I can report on this. I've thought profoundly about how best to approach this, what kind of questions to ask you, how to get you to open up. You are very young. No one wants to believe me. I tell everyone you are all sharing T-shirts, sharing knickers, sharing toothbrushes, sharing beds. That you are little creatures of the night. No one credits me. Now you, you can help me to explain. That you are not 'children'. Children are not children in the way your parents might think. Janey is your lover. I have Nina's testimony.

Mimi sits silent. Then points at Nina.

Mimi Nina wets the bed.

Mrs B Do you, Nina?

Nina goes red.

What does that mean, Mimi?

Mimi She's upset.

Mrs B Are you calling Nina disturbed?

Mimi A bit.

Mrs B So Janey is not your lover and Nina is disturbed?

Mimi Maybe.

Mrs B I don't have you marked down as a liar.

Mimi I'm not a liar.

Mrs B I wouldn't want to mark you up as a liar on main board. Are you a liar?

Mimi Not the way you say it.

Mrs B I can call your parents and explain the love bite to them.

Mimi No, Mrs B.

Mrs B They will want to know when you go home tomorrow. They will see it. I've already billed them for the window you broke.

Mimi You've got it wrong, Mrs B.

Mrs B Well, either she's your girlfriend or she's a bully.

Mimi My girlfriend?

Mrs B You know what a girlfriend is?

Mimi Like a boyfriend.

Mrs B We know you're very bright, Mimi. Aren't you bright?

Mimi Yes.

Mrs B There aren't many girls in this school who can 'catch *and* add up'.
 Mimi . . . do you have sex with Janey?

Mimi Sex?

Mrs B You can . . . now, Mimi. You can cry. Tell me about Janey. I need to hear it from your mouth. Tell us, Mimi, tell us the whole of it.

 Long silence. Mrs B takes off the oven gloves.

Mimi She's a bully.

Mrs B Not a bully in the usual way.

Mimi A bully.

Mrs B Not in the normal way of it.

Mimi She's mean to me.

Mrs B Really?

Mimi She did this, and this and this, Chinese burns, to me as like a joke. I told her not to.

Mrs B Right.

Mimi She goes into my drawers. She reads my letters. She sucks up to the other girls to hurt my feelings. She ignores me. She spreads rumours about me. She tells me she hates my guts.

Mrs B That does sound –

Mimi It's really normal.

Mrs B A normal bully. Janey, your friend.

Mimi She's not my friend, Mrs B.

Mrs B She was your friend.

Mimi In J1.

Mrs B This does affect things. My report.

Mimi Janey's horrid.

Mrs B I gave it a new title.

Pause.

Half of me doesn't believe you.

Mimi It's true.

Mrs B Can you imagine if Janey were expelled for no reason, Mimi?

Mimi She's what you said before – a bully.

Mrs B And you know what that means?

Mimi Yes.

Mrs B A hundred per cent?

Mimi Sorry, Mrs B.

Mrs B It's you we are worried about. Principally. Nina, would you call Janey a bully?

Nina Yes, but . . .

Janey enters uninvited.

Janey I've come to get Mimi.

Mrs B You're just in time.

Janey It's past nine o'clock.

Pause.

Mrs B Sit.

Lights out.
Janey is sitting on top of her large clothes trunk.
Mimi comes out of the trunk singing madly. Laughing.

Mimi
Once in royal David's city
Stood a lowly cattle shed,
Where a mother laid her baby
In a manger for his bed:
Mary was that mother mild,
Jesus Christ her little child.

He came down to earth from heaven,
Who is God and Lord of all,
And his shelter was a stable,
And his cradle was a stall;
With the poor, the scorned, the lowly,
Lived on earth our Saviour holy.

And, through all his wondrous childhood,
He would honour and obey,
Love and watch the lowly maiden
In whose gentle arms he lay:
Christian children all must be
Mild, obedient, good as he.

For he is our childhood's pattern,
Day by day like us he grew;
He was little, weak and helpless,
Tears and smiles like us he knew.

And he feeleth for our sadness,
And he shareth in our gladness.

And our eyes at last shall see him,
Through his own redeeming love;
For that Child who seemed so helpless
Is our Lord in heaven above;
And he leads his children on
To the place where he is gone.

On the last verse, Janey stops staring at Mimi and comes in with a harmony.
    The two girls are surprised they can be beautiful.

Not in that poor lowly stable,
With the oxen standing round,
We shall see him; but in heaven,
Set at God's right hand on high;
When like stars his children crowned,
All in white shall wait around.

Silence.

Janey What's that song about?

Mimi David.

Janey Who the fuck's David?

Mimi Thank fuck they cancelled it.

Janey Thank fucks.

Mimi There's only so many times you can watch Jesus being born.

Pause.

Play something else.

Janey She'll hear us.

Mimi Meh.

Janey goes over to her tape machine and presses play.
The introductory music of 'Everybody Hurts' by REM
sounds. Mimi looks at Janey.

Janey Sorry.

Mimi Did you read my letter? I sent that ages ago. I
wondered where my parents went.

Janey Sorry.

She finds it and gives it to her.

Mimi It doesn't matter.

Janey You can still send it.

Mimi It doesn't matter.

Janey I know you don't want to share with me.

They go to their bunks.
Torches flash up and down. Girls creep around.
Janey rolls over and out of her top bunk onto the
floor. She crosses over to Mimi's bed.

You have to play now. Last game.

Mimi Fuck dead.

Janey They've got my toothbrush, I lost the last three
games.

Mimi No.

Janey No one can beat you.

Mimi I know. Now fuck off.

Janey rips Mimi's duvet off the bed. Mimi doesn't
react but acts asleep. Janey takes the duvet quickly up
to her bunk. Mrs B enters.
The door closes. Everyone is still for a moment and
then the torches flash.
Janey crawls into Mimi's bunk.

Mimi kicks her hard. Janey falls out. She goes and comes back.

Janey They're going to dip my toothbrush in Amy's diarrhoea. Mimi. Fucking play the cards.

Mimi rolls over.

Mimi, Mimi . . . I'm homesick. I feel really homesick.

Mimi It's end of term.

Janey I mean, I don't want to go home.

Mimi I do feel sick when I go home.

Janey Me too.

Mimi I can't eat home food.

Janey Too rich. Too tasty.

Mimi Too rich. Too nice for my tummy.

Janey You're so binny now. I don't want to go home.

Mimi It's just the change. You get used to it.

Janey I wish my parents were divorced like everyone else's.

Mimi turns her head towards her. Janey sits on the floor curled up in Mimi's duvet.

Mimi Give it back.

Janey Please play.

Mimi Give it back.

Janey Please.

Mimi Please.

Mimi grabs a corner of the duvet and pulls it into her bunk. Janey hangs on to the end of it and uses the momentum to pull her into Mimi's bunk.

Mrs B opens the door and watches.
Mimi and Janey lie close.
Mrs B goes.
Janey kisses Mimi's face then her mouth. They kiss.
Nina creeps up to the bed. She peers into the bunk.
She goes and comes back with a torch shining on them.
Nina runs out of the room. Triumphant.

Janey We have to stay together next term.

Mimi I know.

Janey Please share next term. Please.

Mimi OK.

Janey Will you tell Mrs B we want to roomy now?

Mimi I'll tell her, but –

Janey What?

Mimi Nothing.

Janey Mrs B and my parents think I'm bad and you're good.

Mimi You're not bad.

Janey Swear we'll share?

Mimi Don't keep crying.

Janey I don't want to go home.

Mimi I promise you.

They hug. They hold each other.

Marcus drags Mimi's trunk into the two-bed dorm. He goes back out and comes in with her tuck box.

Marcus What happened to your old one?

Mimi shrugs.

Who are you bunking with? It's only got your name on the door.

Mimi Should be Janey.

Marcus Says just you.

Mimi You don't get your own room until you're lower sixth. Not for five years.

Marcus They must have left her name off.

Pause.

Mimi They never do that.

Silence.

Marcus Are all your friends in love with me?

Mimi They like the photos of us in France.

Marcus When I was skiing?

Mimi Yes.

Marcus When it was hot and I had my shirt off?

Mimi I suppose so.

Marcus Did you bring Blu-Tack for your posters?

Pause.

Mimi I think so.

Marcus Phewsh.

Pause.

Mimi I've got one of Brad Pitt and one of a hamster in the wild.

Pause.

Say something.

Marcus There was a boy in my year once who never stopped crying. He'd wake people up. I punched him in the stomach once, because I couldn't sleep. So they put him in a room on his own. He was a nonce.

Mimi Did they?

Marcus For the sake of everyone else.

Mimi Of course.

Marcus I still see him.

Mimi Is he an MP?

Marcus What?

Mimi All your friends want to be MPs.

Marcus He's fine. There's nothing wrong with wanting to be an MP. You don't cry a lot do you?

Mimi Not so anyone can hear me.

Marcus Perfect.

Mimi I do it like this.

She takes a pillow from a bunk and presses her face into it to illustrate how it muffles her sound.

Marcus One of my best pals could cry like this, he'd just make the tears come out of his nose, so people would think he had a cold, or was just sick, not homesick. And then he could have a tissue.

We wee'd on someone once for crying too much!
I don't suppose girls do that.

Mimi No.

Marcus What happens tonight?

Mimi House meeting.

Marcus What time do you have to sign back in to main school on a Saturday?

Mimi By supper.

Marcus Oh.

Mimi I normally have a match.

Marcus So you can't sneak to town for a drink? Or for sweets?

Pause.

Mimi No.

Marcus stretches and looks at his watch.

OK.

Marcus You've got lots to do.

Mimi Course.

Marcus I think they loved seeing you. You mustn't egg them on.

Mimi OK.

Marcus I would say I'd come and take you out for tea, but the tea and scones sort of sit in your stomach, don't they? You just have to get on with it, do very very well in your exams for the next . . . and then, you can do anything you want.

Mimi I want to be a vet.

Pause.

Marcus They care, you know.

Mimi I made a fuss.

Marcus You made a massive fuss.

Mimi I thought the school would call them.

Pause.

Marcus And if you *really* didn't want to be here, they wouldn't make you. They only want the best for you. And you are doing so well. You might end up being a real big shot.

Pause.

Wailing doesn't count.

Mimi I don't want to be a fuck-up.

Marcus You can't be a fuck-up at ten. Once you're done with this, being a junior, you can do anything you like.

Mimi I don't have a roomy.

Marcus . . .

Mimi Bye.

They hug. Marcus leaves. The fire door slams shut.
  Mimi waits. then runs after him. He carries her back in.

Mimi I can't be here on my own. I need to go home, I need to go home. Marcus, please. It's gone wrong, it's gone wrong, it's gone wrong. Please, please, please, please.

Marcus Grow up, Mims.

Marcus smoothes her hair. Then goes.
  Mimi opens her trunk with her key. She gradually unpacks. Four white shirts on a hanger.

Two green V-neck jumpers in the drawer.
Twelve pairs of green socks in the chest of drawers
Games kit in her sports bag (Airtex T-shirt, games
skirt, grey bags, long green hockey socks, trainers,
hooded green jumper).
Lace-up shoes at the bottom of the cupboard.
She takes out an elasticated sheet, puts it on the bed,
crawling over the mattress on her knees. She puts a
red and black duvet cover on her duvet. And does one
pillow.
She unrolls a poster of a hamster and puts it up on
the wall above her bed.
Mimi sits quietly on her own.
Nina rushes in . . .

Nina Sorry, wrong room!

Nina leaves.
Mimi leans over and pushes her face into her pillow.
She takes a pen out of her tuck box.
She opens the wardrobe door. She squares off a
space in the middle and starts to write her name.